The Park Vet

by Greg Frazier
illustrated by Mick Reid

Practice Decodable 50

Mc Graw Hill Education

Bothell, WA • Chicago, IL • Columbus, OH • New York, NY

MHEonline.com

Send all inquiries to:
McGraw-Hill Education
8787 Orion Place
Columbus, OH 43240

ISBN: 978-0-02-138930-8
MHID: 0-02-138930-6

Printed in China.

8 9 10 11 12 DSS 27 26 25 24 23

The kids were at the animal park.
They had adopted a yak.

"Jump in this van," said Val.
"Let's visit the park vet."

"I will tell what cash helps us do," said the vet.

The vet finished telling the kids.
"Thanks for helping," she said.

Val had a gift for the kids.
The kids got park vests!

Yasmin patted the yak.

"I will visit whenever I can," she said.